Flowers In The Margin

© 2018 Jessica Exner. All rights reserved.
978-0-359-25504-7

www.facebook.com/jessica.fing.exner

Cover image by Anthony Haley
www.facebook.com/murmurmonsters

Edited by Josh Poitras
www.facebook.com/justanemptypen

Flowers In The Margin
by Jessica F'ing Exner

"You are strong. I believe in you."

-Carlee

"You are so sweet, Jessica. You are the sweetest person I know."

-Carlee

"So amazing talking today to you! My spirit is lifted big time. Love you so much! You are truly a wonderful friend! And I'm still smiling."

-Carlee

**In the lovingest memory
of my very best friend,
Carlee
my Paper Bag Princess**

There is a section of poems in this collection
titled Rich in Spirit, written in her honour.
Hand-written copies of those poems
can be purchased by donation to
The Canadian Mental Health Association
in Carlees' name.

6

Foreword

When I asked what a foreword should entail, I was given these examples;

> Who is this book for
> Who inspired it
> Who made it what it is

So, it's for the kid's I've created. For them to take with them always, tucked away in their pocket for when I no longer fit.

It's for the 12 year old me, who is sitting sad and afraid.. wondering if she'll ever do something worth talking about... or if she'll even make it long enough to try. If I could do anything I would mail her a letter:

> *You did it!*
> *You made it!*
> *You're amazing!*
> *Yours truly,*
> *You <3*

And for every child left behind by a parents conscious choice. I'm sorry and it's not your fault. Stay strong and build a you that YOU ARE proud of.

And for every set of eyes mine have ever met. If we exchanged a glance, you made a difference in my life.

And for the heart(s) I've broken, I'm truly sorry for the time you spent trying to see the good in me. You tried so hard, but I couldn't find it.

I have found it, and I will forever be grateful for you. The work in this book, in it's entirety, was inspired

7

by love and loss. There are times they come hand in hand, and those are the times that hurt the most. And you will find plenty of that in these pages.

My biggest strength is the same as my largest flaw, I care too much. I give every piece of me to everyone I meet, and most times I've been left piecing it all back together alone. But sometimes, sometimes I'm left with a beauty so pure it makes it all worth it.

Now, the idea and courage to begin production and publishing of this work came to me after a year of sharing my poetry publicly at an event called *The Drunk Poets Society* held locally in Orillia, where I met some of the most amazing writers and performers. It was run then by Mr. Tom Rose. He and the other Drunk Poets created an amazing platform for local poets and aspiring writers like myself to pursue what we deserve to believe in most- ourselves. Tom gave me my first taste of public reading, and I will never look back. So, he is either to thank or to blame, and that is up to you!

However, I am forever grateful for him and his stage presence, and his bomb ass sweater vest collection. So, thank you Tom, and thank your mom, for birthing a famous millennial.

Thank you to my very best friend, Carlee, for believing in me every single day and in every single way. If you ask my girls about their Aunty Car-Car they will tell you she lives in our hearts forever and that their mother is a better person because of her.

And finally, thank you to *Just An Empty Pen – Josh Poitras* for planting the book seed in my mind, and casually watering it when I wasn't paying attention. Thank you for calling me out on all my bullshit, and making me face the things I fear the most about myself. I am a better writer because of you.

Flowers In The Margin
by Jessica F'ing Exner

10

Table of Contents

Rainbows and Butterflies and Shit

Sunshine
Winter Wonderland
JESSICA
Bicycle Race
Second Hand Love
Just An Empty Pen
Drunk Poet

My PTSD & Me

Disappointment
HeartBeat
Dearest Abandoned Family
Disgusting
Once A Little Girl
Easter Baby
Fallen
Don't Smoke
Freight Train
Life Goals
I'm Not Broken
Silence
Grow A Garden
Sixteen Christmas'
Cried To A Stranger
Shame
Hard To Hate You

She

SHE
Anxiety Is
I Don't Kill Myself
Sad Eyes
Live And Learn
Angry
To Do

Sorry Not Sorry

Not Just A Body
Wild Columbine
On The Other Side Of The Phone
Slow It Down
I Will Love You Forever
On A Warm Day
Just Loved
Dear Death
Liar
Some Days
Racial Injustice
Something New
My Haven
Fuck Death
I Guess
Times I Can't Breath
#MeToo
Something I'll Never Do Again
Woman Of Wonder
Physical Repent
I Am Woman
Set A Goal
Disability Is Disability
Sick Of Rhyming

Karma's A Bitch
Girl In The Back
Existence
You Found God
Nonchalant

Gushy Bullshit

Puppy Love
Pushing You Away
Hard to Handle
Am I The Worst
A Bit Different Now
On A Dark & Stormy Night
Fell In Love With A Writer
Hello Fear
Thought Of Leaving You
Universal Signs

Rich In Spirit

Rich In Spirit
Warrior
Paint The Sky
Dreamer
Celebration Of Your Life
Missing You
Rest In Power

Momming is Hard

My Eyes
Netflix And Chill
288 Hours
Lost In Thoughts
Be Better

14

Rainbows
& Butterflies
& Shit

16

Sunshine

Every morning I watch
The sun
Rise above the ground
I sit
I wait
I wonder
And this is what I have found

Every single sunrise is different
Each one holds its own unique
Spray of colours across last nights sky

Every hue
Of every blue
3Some pinks and its friends
Escaping the horizon
And absorbing every bend

And some days its makes
No dramatic appearance at all
Could make you question
If it's chosen to fall

But she's here everyday
No matter how brilliant
Even on the darkest days
She shines anyways

Winter Wonderland

Snowfalls

Skin crawls

As we make our way

He's a good driver

She's a good navigator

But none of that really matters

Cause when one fuck face

Is taking over the place

We'll all end up in a ditch

So drive safe you Fuckers

JESSICA

Just as you

Entered this world

Strength entered your

Soul and

It was never

Contained

Again

Bicycle Race

Sometimes in my dreams I'm driving
But I mean sometimes in my dreams I'm dying
So I don't know how this will sound
But the feeling of drivers freedom I've never actually found

Until
The other day I bought a bike
I fly like a kid again
riding my trike
I peddle that thing all day
And I ride that thing all night

The freedom that came from my first taste
Had tears welling and streaming down my face

Second Hand Love

The perfect shirt
Is already worn in
Faded and thin

Not by me but
My favourite jeans
Have holes in the knees

Do you wonder where
I got them all
It wasn't the mall

Sifting through tops
In all the thrift shops
I love to pass my time

Nothings ever the same
The experience keeps me sane
Searching the perfect find

And the finds fill my home
Summer dresses and garden gnomes
Its all unique and it's all... mine

But your heart is my favourite used item
Worn and torn and left behind
Set neatly is a dusty corner for me to find

Just An Empty Pen

A pen and paper
Feels like it's all I need
Like I'll instantly feel lighter
Move my fingers
And the words will bleed

But I'm stuck
Writing words with no meaning
And I'm stuck
with my courage line receding

It's worse then a bad hair day
Cause I can't pin it back
And failure smells worse then week old laundry
When the quarters lack

The pen keeps on moving
And I'm hoping for the best
Wishing on a shooting start
For something deeper then the rest

But it's not
It's really really not
Just a bunch of thoughts on paper
Rambling words is all I've got
And this pen is the only thing lighter

Drunk Poet

So I did a thing and it was honestly great

I got dressed up and stayed out late

I chatted with some friends

And I didn't want it to end

I shared my poetry once again

With my flowered notebook in hand

And to my favourite crowd

I read it all out loud

I had so much fun

And when it was done

I tucked my kids into bed

And went over it all in my head

I can't explain how grateful I am

To hear others read as well

Because if it weren't for them

I'd have never have read myself

24

My PTSD & Me

26

Disappointment

Disappointment comes

In all shapes and colours

The worst is in the form

Of a father or a mother

HeartBeat

"You know what her heart sounds like
From the inside"

But I don't remember
All I've got are memories
Of being sad in December

And all the times I was stranded

Begging for love
And left empty handed

Dearest Abandoned Family

I left behind some friends of mine
Walked away without giving a damn

Packed up those pieces in my travellers bag
And where no on knows is where my heart grows

I found some peace that secured my pieces

Though I've never unpacked
Cause my courage lacked

So here I'm going to tell me story
Not to brag and for no glory

I'm unaccepted
Constantly corrected
Questioned and wondered
Or used and abused

As a child
I'd have gone anywhere
And as a teen
I'd have done anything

To find it

And I didn't know what it was
And I found a lot of things
before I found me

I wore someone else' ring
At the age of seventeen

My time in the streets
Was safer inside

Then being at home

Between an older mans sheets
Thinking I was old enough to know

No regrets, they say
It's an easy way to live

If you refuse to grow
To learn
To realize
To wish
You could have gone home

What left do I have to give
Beating myself down is all I've ever known
Denying my body
Taking time on loan

Just waiting to be
Older
Better
Wiser

So what now you ask
Cause here we are
Well now
I'll do what I've always done

I'll keep up
I'll take what I've learned
And I'll soldier on

Disgusting

I feel absolutely disgusting right now
I'd like to feel better, but I don't know how

I couldn't even explain if wanted to
But mostly because I'm not interested in
The list of shit you think I should do

Like... "get out of my head"
Yeah, cause that's fucking possible

Or maybe... "think positively".. sure
Even though reality is fucking unstoppable

It's not your house that's a mess
Because of your neglect
It's mine

It's not your mind
Forcing time to reflect
It's mine

And they're not your sorrows
Drowning in a pool of regret
They're mine

So, don't
For a fucking second
Try to assure me, that
"All will be fine"

Once a Little Girl

I was once a little girl

Surrounded by fear and tears

And not a whole lot has changed

After thirty years

Except that

I'm no longer yours

Easter Baby

Are you the Easter Baby
Said some strange lady

At the recent funeral for my
Uncle D
The guy who holds the
The standards I seek
In the man of my dreams

Well this woman was at my birth
And goes on to say
She was with my Uncle watching
A big hockey game that day

It was 1987
Islanders Vs. Capitols
It was game 7
When he heard my Ma' was in hospital

This woman's name is Rebecca
Becky for short
And this story she's telling
Is filling my heart

She tells me they get to the hospital
And the frantic search begins
"Find my sister!" he says to her
And he finds a TV to see who wins

It's an easy search for her
And his was a frantic mess
I left my mother waiting 36 hours
So Becky never knew my name was Jess

Cause after 4 periods of overtime
And the Islanders won the game
They all fell asleep, or left
Before I was given my name

Except my Uncle Dan of course
And a few others who rode out
The 36 hour course

Sigh
Huh... the Easter baby
It's nice to have a title

Sigh
Its nice to have a story

Fallen

I have fallen
I can't get up
The weight is
More then I
Can carry

I have fallen
I try to get up
My arms buckle
My legs shake
This is scary

I have fallen
About to give up
I'm ready
To lay here
And be buried

I have fallen
I have to get up
I have to get up
But I'm not moving
Now I'm worried

Don't smoke

7 years old
Mom found me smoking in the yard
Punishment
Smoke a whole pack till I barf

Only thing she could think of I suppose
I remember how badly it burned my nose

Then 13 hanging out by the bushes in the street
Since my home life was shaky and incomplete

I took a drag of that cigarette
And man I remember the instant regret

Like, why would anyone chose to do this

As that cigarette made its second way around
Since smokes back then were hardly found

My mom pulled up in her big fancy truck
Busted me smoking, just my luck

I was thinking of never doing it again
But at this point in my life
Smoking may make my mom my friend

So when she asked if I liked it
I lied and complied
Told her I did and I wasn't gonna stop

I was hoping it would get me on her priority list
Right there at the top
And it worked

She bought me smokes in lieu of education
Oh and to watch the baby do the laundry
Clean the house and of course
Don't answer the phone

Heaven forbid someone find out
About your lack of dedication
And the fact that we're alone

I don't know where she got the truck
Could have been Bill, or Joe... maybe even Chuck

But we'd smoke late at night on the porch
Hiding from my step dad of course
Cause my Mom'd get torched
Letting her young daughter smoke

I'm 30 now, well 30 and a half
It's hard to breath and I cough when I laugh

I'm still smoking though
But it's less to fit in
It's more of an itch
I get under my skin

Freight Train

Thoughts running through
Like a fucking freight train

Seems like weeks
It's been pissing rain

Blocked by my minds barrier
And nothings unfolding
What happened to that little girl warrior

It's soon to be morning
Yet here we are

Another sleepless moon
And daylight comes to soon

Life Goals

I always had a goal
Made a promise to my soul
That I would hit the age of thirty
And I would do it completely drug free

I couldn't by my mother
And I refused to be my father

It feels to soon
But I'm almost thirty-one
And non the less
Here she comes

The mid-life mom
With no time for fun
Between birthday parties
And doctor appointments
We're always on the run

I don't know what I would change though
If anything at all
Maybe just being so afraid
That one day I'm bound to fall

He says I'm thirty
And It's to late to break
But he has no Idea
That this strength is entirely fake

That everyday
No matter how hard I try
And even though I've never been
I think about what it might be like
To get high

I'm Not Broken

I'm not broken

But I am breaking

I knew it when

My heart started racing

I'm not yet shattered

But everything is shaking

And I know I'll never reach

The solidity I'm chasing

Silence

Growing up I was silent

And anyone anyone who knew me then
Will laugh when they hear me say that now

Since I never shut up

I could always find something to talk about
Telling jokes
Telling stories
Terribly never ending

But I was silent

When speaking up should have mattered
I kept my mouth shut in situations that scared me

I let myself go out of fear

When I should have had the strength to hold on
My voice was loud and funny and vibrant
But quiet and subtle and cowardly

So I'm making a change

I'm done walking around like I'm not worth anything
Like you shouldn't be thrilled to me smiling in the street

I'm finished being afraid to stand here
Being afraid to sing
Like I can't shatter stone with the strength in my feet

Refuse to remain
Refuse the shame
Refuse any terms
Refuse and stand firm

It's not just me anymore I'm raising little children
Two tiny little me's and all I want for them is courage
For their dreams to never be discouraged

And they're watching my every move
And judging how to make theirs
From the clothes they wear
The way the react and how they do their hair

So I'm done caring about the people
I don't even know
And I'll take take the compliments from
The hearts that I grow

Grow a Garden

I want to grow a garden

But the soil is beginning to harden

I dig and I dig

But nothing prevails

I'll just keep watering

And when all else fails

I'll find a new patch of dirt

To bury all my hurt

Sixteen Christmas'

Sixteen Christmas'
Watching you craft, wrap
And decorate

Sixteen Christmas'
Spent ignoring you
Pretending to be great

Sixteen Christmas'
Like sixteen seasons
Of a rotten TV show

Bad actors and false hope
For a bright new year

Sixteen Christmas'
Wondering while you
Made the house glow

Where did you find all this
Goddamned holiday cheer

This was fourteens Christmas'
Since I woke up with you

Fourteen Christmas'
That I've struggled to live through

I was the Grinch who hated Christmas
For a few short years

And then woke with random family members
And shed some good tears

I've spent Christmas
With the Nana that you hid from me

And spent Christmas with your Ex
And decorated our old family tree

And when I decided it was time
To start my own traditions
I started by building my own family

So here we are
Just me and my kids
Who don't know you
Ad I'm a committed mom
The whole year through

Cried to a Stranger

I cried to a complete stranger today
And that comes as no surprise
I know

Tears started
When I started
To explain
My reasoning
And questioning
To stay or go

Why I'm in this little town
And who I've lost
I could always run away
But at what cost

I'm staying
And I'm praying
To my warrior princess
Let this be my place
My time
To finally rest

Shame

Shame stains my face

As I do my best to replace

The trust I stole from you

When I questioned your truth

But not much else can be expected

From a heart that feels rejected

Hard To Hate You

It's so hard to hate you
And believe me I've tried

It should be so easy
After all the times you've lied

But there's something about you
that makes hating you feel wrong

And I think it's the fact that
You're supposed to be my mom

The one trusted soul
To run to when things get rough

I've spent so many years
Trying to forget you
It's been tough

Cause no matter how hard
I try to push you away
I still think of you with love

She

50

SHE

She..

She is...

She is anxiety

The alternative opinion
The voice that doesn't let me sleep

She is...

Diluted intentions

Downed in salt water tears
And forever caged

She is..

An inner daemon

Abandoned in a field of fears
And fully enraged

She is..

Me

Anxiety Is

Anxiety is a bullied conscious

That comforting voice of reason
The one the ones you love

Planted for you

Repeated kind words into your mind as a babe
Told you all the things you'd need to know

And how to cope when you don't

You hear it when you're loved lost or alone
Reminders of where you're supposed to be

When and why

Well mine
Mines a bitch
And she talks a lot of shit

About me
About my every move

She makes irrational real
Unknowing becomes ungoing

Worst of all, she a confused little twit
And everything I'm doing is wrong

And if you listen careful

You can hear its my mom

Sixteen plus years
She embedded herself in my mind

Like most mothers do

But mine dropped a poison
And fed it as it grew

So watch your words to the one's you grow

Cause come one day it's all they'll know

I don't kill myself

I don't kill myself
Instead I stay neatly inside
Where my shattered heart can hide

I don't kill myself
But instead remove myself
From the world that would make it so easy

The world that makes me feel sleazy
See she tells me often

That this could all be over
If I let her take the wheel

She constantly reminds me
Of all my mistakes
And how they truly make me feel

And she can take control
If I give her that role
And this could all be over

Sad Eyes

She's here again
Swollen eyes
And sad goodbyes

Hands are shaking
This smile I'm faking

She's such a fucking bitch
And she brings along that awful twitch

The twitch that's constantly dropping the ball
The one that carefully builds those walls

The 10 foot walls surrounding
My good intentions
Suffocating me in my lifes
Reflections

No windows and no doors
And there's no way out
No one is here to help
And there's no one to hear my shouts

My screams are echoing through
This awful place
And once again I'm praying to the universe
I find my saving grace

Live and Learn

"Live and learn"
"Just wait your turn"

Don't tell me what I need

I turn around
and hit the ground

And out my soul will bleed

It comes and goes
And don't you know

That's where sorrow breeds

In that place
Without a face

Her job is almost complete

She's come with a task
To take of my mask

And show the world I'm a cheat

I'm all kinds of fake
And there's not much I can take

She leaves every part of me weak

Angry

Angry

Paranoid

Anxious

Sad

Mean

Hurt

Angry

Depression is a son of a bitch

Got your insides burning

And making you wish

It could all just end

Or maybe

You could find a friend

In yourself

Take your heart and soul

Down from that shelf

The one behind the encaging walls

The locks

The keys

The gate keeper begs

And she pleads

For you too feed

Her a part of these

Pieces of you

She waits patiently

For your mind to fall

And be buried away

With these

Pieces

Of you

To Do

She's made a list
Of all the things
I might have missed
When I considered
How
Why
Where
Did it go wrong

60

Sorry Not Sorry

62

Not Just A Body

I'm not just a body

I'm a beautiful soul

With an open mind

And there's still

So much of this world

For me to find

Wild Columbine

My little apartment
Almost downtown
She on the very top floor
And I
Tucked neatly on the ground

Main door entrance
First time I saw her face
She left me in a trance
Spiralling yet stuck in place

Beautiful doesn't seem right
It was more then that
It was moons and stars lost in the night
She was a goddess in a grimy city flat

A Wild Columbine
Blooming through the steel
A gloomy days sunshine
Too alluring to be real

And she wanted me
Me
Could she not see
That I was just
Me

I had not much to offer
No previous experience
But she let me love her

And I did. I really did

Right up until its bitter end
She took from me
What she got from all her friends

I wish I had resisted

But she was a Wild Columbine
Blooming through the steel
A gloomy days sunshine
Too alluring to be real

On The Other Side Of The Phone

You used your words
like they held no meaning

Tore me apart slowly
When you saw me beaming

My ship still sailed
After all failed attempts

How
After all those years
Being held in contempt

You loaded your cannons
With ammo loaned in our time together

Shot away proudly
With hopes to destroy me forever

And for a moment
Longer then I'd like to admit

You had me down
For I had been hit

A whole in my heart
And the ache poured in

Destroying the beauty
Before it could even begin

But see the thing about your words is
I have them all
And I'll see you in court

Slow it Down

I'm learning to slow it down

That not every answer

Needs to be found

I'm learning to be steady

After so many years

I'm finally ready

To take my time

And enjoy what's mine

I Will Love You Forever
I Will Like You For Always

I am made of stardust
I am made of love
I am built of moon powder and dreams
That fit like a glove

It's not easy to say goodbye
To someone you've never met
And how you can say
It's better this way
Is something I'll never get

Your words ring
"Now is not the time"
And maybe that's true

But my reactions
And how I feel about it
Isn't up to you

My body is a temple
Yet it can't grow a seed
"Be happy with the two you have"
Don't tell me what I need

I've held baby number 4
And I've kissed baby number 6
I love these babes
But my feelings are mixed

So to baby 1, 2, 3, 5 and 7
You're the only reason
I believe in a Heaven

As long as I'm living
My Babies You'll be
Time I Can't Breath

There's time I feel

Like I can't breath

Like all the weight

Is pushing down on me

And sometimes though

Are my favourite times

On A Warm Day

If she came by

On a warm sunny day

And vocalized all the things

You need her to say

That she'd pick up

In all the places she once lacked

Would you consider

Even for a second

Taking her back

Just Loved

I just want to be loved
Is that so much to ask

It seems to be accepting of me
Is such an ungodly task

"You're not enough"

"Girl you're to much"

But I'm just right in the middle
Patently waiting

Apparently surrounded by riddles
No one can solve

Dear Death

Dear death

Give it a rest

I've lost count of your visits this year

But you must have hit your quota my dear

You've come more then I'd like to admit

And I can't put out this fire you've lit

LIAR

Lies

Liar

You're a liar

One way or another

Fucking lies

It was all a lie

All your words

Said or text

Lies

You're a liar

A coward

And a Liar

Some Days

Some days are harder then others
They say all we need is each other

But my bed is where I'd like to be
My bed allows my emotions to be free

No one telling me how to feel
And I can just pretend
None of this is real

That you're still hanging around
Even though I know
You're nowhere to be found

Racial Injustice

How do I write about racial injustice
When I don't even know where I stand

Should I be begging for forgiveness
Like
Am I just a white girl with blood on my hands

I want to fight the racial war
But afraid to look like a fool
My grandma wrote a book
Back when I was school

Shared all my paternal family
And from where in which they came
But I was 22 when I learned
My story wasn't the same

I have no answers and I have no fuel
And what if my bloodline broke the rules

So I spit in that fancy little tube
And I'll wait for results
I'm hoping for peace of mind
In my glory or for my faults

Something New

I wanted to write something new

A piece that is uncontrollably true

And all I've come up with

Is how ridiculously hard it is

To keep on living with out you

My Haven

My time in Green Haven
Was short and sweet

Left my heart
Feeling incredibly complete

The women

Their strength

Had my soul searching at great lengths

I found something there
I thought I had lost

And it came at and absolutely
beautiful cost

The woman and the mother
I am so supposed to be

Fuck Death

Fuck death

And what it steals

Fuck loss

And how bad it feels

I Guess

I guess it's time that

I learn how

To hold back my feelings now

I fell so quick

So fast

Without any reassurance

That it would last

#MeToo

There's something happening
Scars are being revealed

Its heart breakingly beautiful
As the victims are beginning to heal

So now I'm going to touch base
On the hashtag MeToo

And you might be uncomfortable
As I tell a story that's true

In June of a year I'd rather not say
I agreed to participate in a date

He's supposed to pick me up
And we'd drive to a friends

And unfortunately that's not
How this story ends

The guy showed up and claimed he had to pee
So I did the kind thing and told him to follow me

To my apartment door
The one nicely placed up on the fifth floor

And I showed him where to go
And little did I know

He'd show up behind me
When my hands were full
And take what wasn't his

And the ending starts like this

He text me the next day
And asked if I'd enjoyed his stay

But I'm the one ashamed
Cause I met him online
So what exactly
Was I expecting

Something I'll Never Do Again

Pretty sure that's something I'll never do again

Where exactly were you when I needed a friend

Busy

Distracted

Annoyed

I'm not blind

And now my own strength is hard to find

Woman of Wonder

I am not Wonder Woman
But a woman of wonder

A woman who craves falling rain
And the crackles of thunder

A woman who enjoys laughter for no reason
Who cares
Who screams and
Who's anger can make her indecent

I am a woman who feels

With every inch of her being

That there's more to this life
That what you and I can seeing

Physical Repent

Yesterday was the first
You saw me at my worst

And today is just the same
As I refuse to say your name

I'm going to push you away
In hopes that you'll stay

I'm sick bud
I didn't lie
And this has nothing to do
With that last guy

This is my body
The one that's "strong"
I told you from the beginning that that was wrong

That I was weak
From my mind to my feet

My guts shake and my mind fakes
Emotional content

I Am Woman

I am woman

Hear me roar

If you don't like it

There's the door

Set A Goal

I set a goal to put words out

Every single day

But today I'm feeling lost

Without a whole lot to say

My feelings are confused

And words seem overused

Disability Is Disability

I'm feeling cold and weak
And a bit incomplete
As the sickness takes over my body

Feeling tired and bleak
From my mind to my feet
And my figure and face are ungodly

Disability is disability
Whether you see it or not
And an auto-immune disease is what I've got

So as I unkempt as I am
From time to time
Or as well as I am
And you think I'm "just fine"

My body is mine
And I'll watch for the signs
While you keep
Your opinions to yourself

Sick of Rhyming

I'm so sick of rhyming

Repeating lines with perfect timing

I'd like to just share exactly how I feel

And I'd like for it to somehow sound real

Karma's A Bitch

Karma is a bitch babe

Just you wait and see

I'm not even worried Love

Cause she ain't coming for me

Girl In The Back

To the girl in the back

Wearing all black

Cause it makes her look
A little "less fat"

FUCK THAT
You're perfect

To the boy over there

Worrying to much about his hair
Cause he thinks that everyone cares

FUCK THAT
You're perfect

To my arms
You're perfect

To my gut
You're perfect

To my hair that dries how ever it wants

The pimples from my new birth control

And the way my thighs

High five

Every time I walk by

It's all fucking perfect

Existence

It would be so much easier

If you had never existed

Easier to accept

then being black listed

Pretending we never knew

Never touched

Never grew

Like we never loved

One another

And each other

You found god

You found God
That's great honestly
I'm happy for you

He's forgiven all your sins
You say
And so now you can too

That's great honestly
I'm so happy for you

You must be sleeping well at night
Now that you're winning that internal fight

That's great honestly
I'm really happy for you

I mean I'm one of those sins
But thank heavens you've been forgiven

For that time you left me for an hour
And came back three days later

And that time you got caught behind the mall
Giving that cop a favour

Oh and when you heard my plea for a better life
You ignored my attempts and continued your role as a wife

Or the smacks in the face
That left my jaw out of place

That's great honestly
I'm happy for you

I'm so glad Gods forgiven the things that you've done
To me

I guess I should be sleeping well at night
Since Gods forgiven you
Right

Nonchalant

On this side it feels
Like you're keeping up an appearance

Not entirely committed
And not willing to allow me clearance

Holding on just enough
To keep me entertained

And letting go just enough
To keep my feelings strained

Gushy Bullshit

96

Puppy Love

It's hard to write when I'm happy
Can't stand the thought of being sappy
And anyone who knows me knows
I don't write about boys

But I met a man
and he's done something to me
I'm pretty sure anyone paying attention can see

I'm laughing more

He's been taking care of my mind
And even though puppy love is unbearable
This shits been growing over time

I'm smiling more

And I hate that I'm so happy
Cause everything's coming out sappy

Pushing You Away

I'm pretty sure I'm pushing you away
Not on purpose of course

But I have no control of the things I say
Not on purpose of course

I'm not ready for you to leave
Not on purpose of course

I'm not sure I'd know hot to grieve
Not on purpose of course

I want to trust you
I want to love you

I need to trust you
I need you to love me too

And I know I have to do it on purpose

I'm Sorry and I cant say it enough

Just please don't give up on this

Hard to Handle

I'm a lot to handle this I know
I'm sick and I'm twisted
And this courage is all for show

All I'm saying is
I wouldn't be surprised
If you decide
To let me go

Like if you've come to terms with the fact
That I'm not your best investment from 2017
If you're gonna do it though
Please don't be to mean

Could you please leave my heart
Some where easy to find
I don't want to search to hard
For comfort and resolution

And I can't be held responsible
To come to healthy conclusions

So

One last time
I'll give you the chance

To get out now
While you still can

Am I the Worst

Am I the worst
For being unsure
And confused about his intentions

I carelessly moved walls
Rearranged the barriers
Made a maze

For him to find his way

But his walls still stand sturdy

I've never felt so insecure

I'm used to being overly unsure

But this confidence in him
Has got me confused
And questioning the truth

I'm used to men
Who are mean and unclean

Respectless and moralless

With fake assurances of who they are
And what they have

But him he's something fucking special man
Pretty sure I'm his biggest fan

A Bit Different Now

It's a bit different now
When I read your words

Fear of embarrassment
Keeps me from gushing

And even though we're moving fast
It doesn't feel like rushing

I've been listening to your soul now
For what almost a year

And i think its kinda funny how
It's helped curb my lovely fears

But now when I read your work
I feel more my heart aches for you

And as you've slept next to me
I've cried as I've wondered

What did that evil bitch do
How could anyone
Ever
Be so cruel to you

On A Dark Stormy Night

When the rain is falling
Thunders cracking
And lightning strikes

The broken trees
Are falling around you
And all you can find is night

You're scared
And alone
And so far
From home

But home
Is where
Your heart is

And your
Heart is deep
In my pocket

Tucked away with
Ticket stubs
Late nights
And laughter

And that
Sweet boy
Can be your
Happily Ever After

Fell In Love With A Writer

I fell in love with a writer

But he doesn't write about me

He only jots about heart ache

And the torture that it brings

Hello Fear

Hello fear

Fancy meeting you here

In my happy place

It's no surprise you'd show your face

It's what you do best

Do you ever rest

Take time of

A little vay-cay

As the basic bitches say

I'm sure we could all use a bit of a break

Cause anyone not afraid to fall in love

Is a fake

Thought of leaving you

I thought of leaving you today
But if you asked me why
I'm not sure what I would say

That I am a coward
and can't cope with the unknown

that I am still unsure of your intentions
even after all the compassion you've shown

Or maybe it's the scenarios
I've created out of nothing
the ones where you're a fake
and every part of you is bluffing

Universal Signs

I'm gonna write some lines
About all my favourite times
The universe said that you should be mine

January 2017
An event I'd never been
And I face that couldn't be seen

Your voice over the crowd
I heard it clear and loud
But your face could not be found

At the bar I sat with my hands in my lap
Then catching glimpses of a baseball cap
Over heads of strangers as we excitedly clapped

And there was a time or two
After this
That I thought of you

And again in March of that year
I came right back unknowingly to hear
More of you and it brought me to tears

That night you changed me personally
I was right where I needed to be
I was opening my eyes to the courage in me

The willingness to be a better more realistic writer
And the strength to continue this life as a fighter

If you weren't you I would have never volunteered my voice
There was something pulling me to make that choice

It was never about being yours
It was just about you
About being proud of
And encouraged by what you do

Then came K Val in July

And I gained the gull to apply

I failed
Of course
But glad I tried

My sister was in town
And I wanted to seem profound

So I bought two tickets

We dressed all nice
And we rode our bikes

I didn't know at first
That you would be there
And I don't remember when
I figured it out to be fair

But you were
With a merch table
And my soul all of a sudden
Was willing and able
To talk to you

It was never about being yours
It was just about you

About being proud of
And encouraged by what you do

We read together again when
You chose me out of that crowd and
I was way more nervous then

And when it was September
The details are harder to remember
I was as cold as December

You were there
And you were kind
I was broken and sad
And a smile was hard to find
But you did

"We should be friends like on the Facebook"
and that night I was gifted your book

My grieving heart
Found a place to fall apart
And a place to be put back together again
And that was the night we became "real friends"

It was never about being yours
It was just about you
About being proud of
And encouraged by what you do

And finally in November
A night I'll always remember

I almost didn't make it
You said your heart couldn't take it

I had no courage to read that night and I had to fake it
So I did
And as I tried to apologize to the crowd
You yelled that I didn't have to so loud
So I didn't I just read
All those terrible thoughts from my head

A big night for us both invited to be the main events
I shared my excitement with you first
And interrupted yours out of strict Poitras thirst

It was never about being yours
It was just about you
About being proud of
And encouraged by what you do

But when you said you knew my heart
Explained your younger life and her part
Something changed
And it could never be the same

The universe handed me this list
Explained that everything had lead to this

This moment
It became about being yours
It was always about you
I'm so incredibly proud of
And encouraged by
Everything you do

110

Rich In Spirit

112

Rich In Spirit

She was

Rich in spirit

And I still feel it

In every part of me

I find comfort

In my weeping heart

Knowing that she's free

Free

Of the hurt she held

And the weakness that she felt

Warrior

I've lost someone who
Was incredibly special to me

And for anyone who's looking
Its so easy to see

I'm not taking it well

My heart is breaking
With every breath

Her soul was brilliant and kind
And brighter then the rest

I'm really not taking it well

So why am I up here
Sharing my story with you all

Because she always believed in me
And I need you to know

That even warriors fall

Paint the Sky

I want to paint the sky
Just one more time
with you by my side

I wanna write about you without rhyming
Without feeling like one emotion has to mend into another

Because they don't

They swirl around with no direction

lost like me

I wanna speak about you without timing
I wanna somehow word the love we had for each other

But I wont

I'll roam around with no direction

Lost like you

Dreamer

Mornings hurt the most
Cause I've spent the nights with you
Lost in the dream lands
Causing havoc like we used to

Chasing tequila and boys
Riding the stars and making noise
Oh how we dance under a moonlit sky
We're loved and free and we're lost in time

Or we sit with the candles lit
Sharing stories from before our solidarity
Gaining a little more familiarity

So I'm begging the sun to rest just a little longer
I'd have you build me up
Cause you make me stronger

Remind me again you know my true beauty
That I am not my mother
I am not the mistakes of my father

But see
That's where I'm wrong
Because you are the sun

So I'll strip myself down
Let my true colours show

Shine your light through
My diamond heart
And I'm a rainbow

Celebration Of Your Life

Yesterday was beautiful
So much Love

The sun was shining
The breeze was wild

You were there

As our friends sang for you
Gypsy birds flew above us
And ants crawled on my toes

You were there

While I lay in the moonlit grass
Crying in the arms of our friend
The stars shined so bright

You were there

And as I sit and contemplate
My emotions of yesterdays
Bitter beauty

You are here

Thank you to your mother
For blessing my life with a light
That will never stop shining

Missing you

A list of things I'd like to say
About my little life
The normal day to day

But I can't

Some really funny shit I'd like to share
Or some sappy junk
When I need someone to care

But I can't

The girls are growing and getting older
The seasons are changing
And I'm getting a bit colder

There's all these little things I notice in the mundane
And all these filthy little secrets
That bring me to shame

But you'll never be home
I'll never reach you by phone

You're just the shadow I can't focus on
And your voice is in the wind

You're these tears that I'm choking on
And the quiver in my chin

Rest In Power

They've been saying rest in peace
But it's never seemed right
Cause you're not resting girl
Your soul was made to fight

I can't say for sure where you've gone
So I'll believe what ever I need
Maybe you're here walking around
Or looking up at the stars with me

Or maybe your soul
Is travelling the world
Visiting all your favourite places

Spreading love and peace
I will always believe
You're putting smiles on strangers faces

But I guess you could be resting
Somewhere with a view

Looking over all the souls that still mourn you
In a tall vine covered
Dragon guarded tower

My sweet paper bag princess
May you rest in power

120

Momming Is Hard

122

My Eyes

Its six AM and the suns not up
But my daughters are

So I rub my eyes real hard

Stumble to the sink
For a cold water splash

And I'm hopin'
They open

They're so heavy and I can barely see
But these two little girls are pulling on me

They've got their first breakfast routine down pat
An apple some grapes or a frozen waffle snack

Just let mommy brew her coffee
Tell me all about your beautiful dreams

And I'll try to listen
As this water thickens

Uh-huh
Oh yeah
Mhmm I say
As I try to give as much
Attention as I can pay

The pot is hot, the cup is clean

I start pouring and I can taste the steam

Take a sip
Sigh
Take another
Sigghh

Alright world I'm ready to mother

Ouu and look
My eyes are open

Netflix And Chill

Just go to bed

Do you know what time it is

It's time for Mommy to
Netflix and Chill

With a bowl of popcorn
And a list of good intentions

Its time for an hour of course words
And bad choices

It's time for me to have a shower

And time to pretend to clean our home

PLEASE just go to bed

Do you get it now

Who's time this is

288 hours

Tell me again how much
Better he is
Then me

And I will remind myself
That's just what
You see

Forty-eight hours out of three hundred thirty-six
And you could never know how badly you're missed

But it's a good time right
No early morning fights

There's no school day dread
And there's not dinner or bed

You do as you please so the day runs with ease
And I'm the only one yelling I know

Cause you're constantly telling me so

Lost in Thoughts

Lost in thoughts of her

And how she ruined me

Blissfully distracted by the weight

Of a little head resting on my feet

And anothers' little hand

Placed gently over mine

Forced to be reminded

That everything is fine

Be Better

My oldest daughter always says

She wants to grow up to be just like me

But I don't know if I will let her

See whenever she says this to me

As flattered as I am

I always tell her

I want her to be better

130

All I've ever wanted to be was a grown-up, a good choice making older person, and I did everything I could to get there.

When I left home the first time I felt like I was just being rebellious, just making a mess of an already messy situation.

I have family to thank for keeping me housed and loved and on the strait and narrow.

But, I think I have to take some time to thank myself, for never wanting to be a dirt bag. Keeping these ridiculous standards for my life and where I wanted it to go. I never wanted to be a doctor or a scientist, I just wanted to be alive.

I wanted so badly to be a good choice making older person.

I've made mistakes.. damn have I made many a mistake...... For a good chunk of my life, sorry to all those who witnessed and thanks to all those who stayed, I expected the good choice making to just kind of come with getting older... I remember the revelation like..."OHHHHHHH.... being a grown-up doesn't just make you a good person!!!!!". It came after many failed attempts at trusting and loving and caring for people who wanted nothing to do with my growth.

I still make mistakes with trust, but one thing I have learned in this process of word writing and book making, is that I trust myself. And if and when shit (havoc) hits the fan (life) I will still be here. . . Ready and able to pick up the pieces and put myself back together again. And again. And again if needed. Because, like the god awful commercials I hated as a child due to lack of understanding, I am fucking worth it.

I have so many people to thank for making this book possible, let alone a FUCKING reality.

My publisher and current love maker, *Just An Empty Pen- Josh Poitras,* who's own amazing poetry and writing can be found on social media by the same name.

Before we were love makers we were common interest companions. We met at a local monthly poetry event called *The Drunk Poets Society* held here in Orillia.

I've seen him pour his guts out and casually pick them up, dust them off and carry on. He's been encouraging me as a writer before I even knew his name.

His first published poetry collection *"My Worthless-Heart"* was gifted to me by Alex Andrews, who then was just a pretty face in a place of faces but has since become an asset to my strength and courage in writing and reading. She gifted me this when my best friend passed away, and it gave me everything I needed to make my way through the suffering and suffocation of loss.

His current Project *Blossom In Winter* is a compilation of poems submitted through and online promotion he put together in hopes to create, publish and sell for the benefit of a worthy charity. He has since, found a wide selection of amazing and aspiring poets, and teamed up with *Smash The Stigma Canada.* I am honoured to have been asked to provide three of my pieces for this cause. "My Eye's", "You Found God" and "Wild Columbine" were submitted with pleasure.

The cover of this book was perfectly created by the artist Anthony Haley. I contacted him knowing he had created the cover of *"My Worthless Heart"*, which had had such an impact of the past year of my life, and being an artist and designer from Hamilton Ont. my home city, referenced in some of these pages, I was honoured when he accepted my request.

Based on the very ridiculous and unprofessional way my request was worded, I was completely blown away when he created exactly what I needed. He is incredibly talented to say the least.

There was most definitely crying when it was first sent to me. So many tears of excitement. And a feeling I honestly can't explain because I've never felt it before. It was like reality was finally beautiful all the way around.

Like the thread of dread weaved through my insides, had finally snapped.

She didn't ring her bell of destruction. She sat back and let it happen, she let me take it all. She allowed my breath to enter and leave my lungs with ease. And she's been pretty quiet since.

So Thank you Anthony, from the roots of my being, for helping create the most beautiful life I have ever experienced.

His amazing creations can be found on social media @anthonyhaleyart & @murmurmonsters, and his creations vary from hand drawn creatures to a hand painted clothing line.
Please just do me the favour of checking him out!!

And now, to the warriors and believers;

My Sisters

I'm proud of each and every one of you, and inspired by your courage and strength every single day. And there are no words to express my love and admiration for the grace you carry tucked neatly in your back pocket while you kick life's ass.

If life were a card game, we'd be playing "Go Fish" with a deck of singles. Our hands over flowing with the fish we've had to pick up. Luckily for us, we know fish can be eaten and cards were only meant to build houses.

We all have our differences, but the one we will all always have the same is each other. Sorry for the corniness, you know how I roll.

To my parents, for making me.

And my fake parents for loving me when they couldn't.

My Grandmother and Grandfather Lambert for knowing my broken bloodline and limitlessly loving me regardless and keeping me humble AF..

Thank you to my children for thinking I'm cool.. hoping it lasts.

And finally... a big glorious thank you to YOU! For reading, maybe laughing, possibly crying, but most importantly just for being you.

<u>You are F'ing PERFECT.</u>